Contents

Birthday parties

People celebrate
their birthdays
in many cultures.

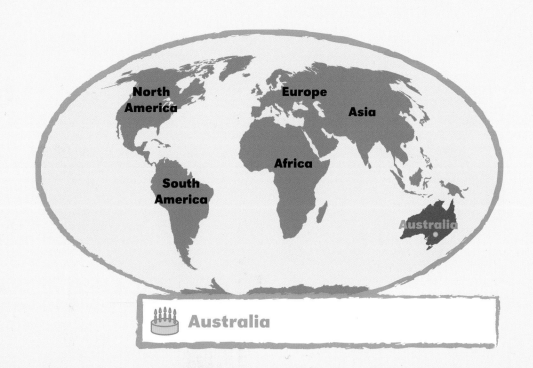

North America

South America

Europe

Africa

Asia

Australia

🎂 Australia

People play games
on their birthdays.
A girl in Mexico
breaks open a piñata.

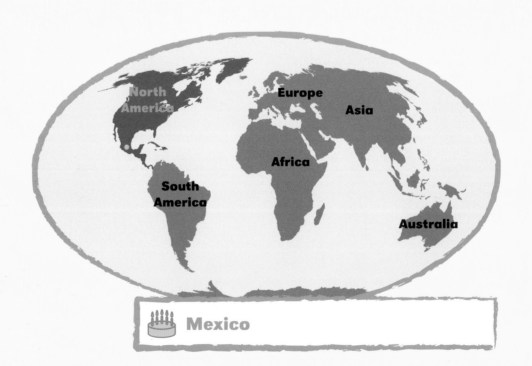

Mexico

A girl in the United States
ducks for apples
at her birthday party.

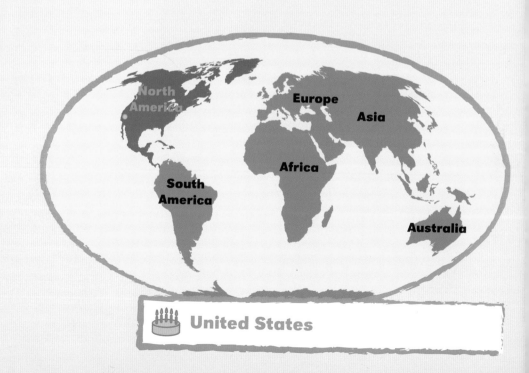

United States

A boy in Sweden
has breakfast in bed
to celebrate his birthday.

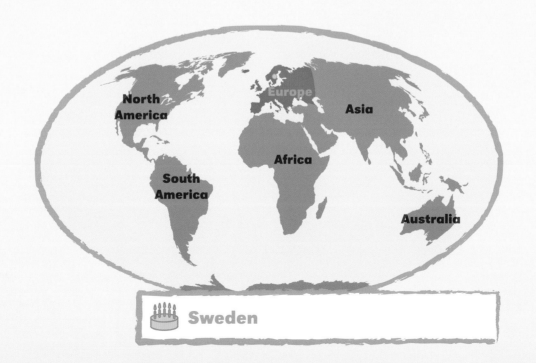

North
America

Europe

Asia

Africa

South
America

Australia

Sweden

More birthday fun

A boy in South Africa
blows out candles
on his birthday cake.

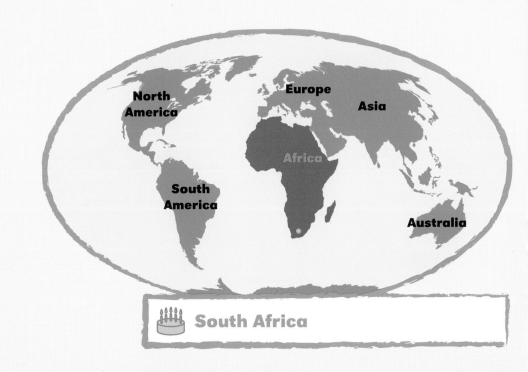

South Africa

A boy in England
goes shopping
on his birthday.

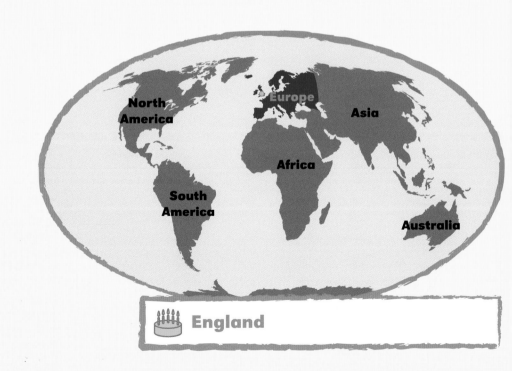

England

A boy in Germany

eats at a restaurant

on his birthday.

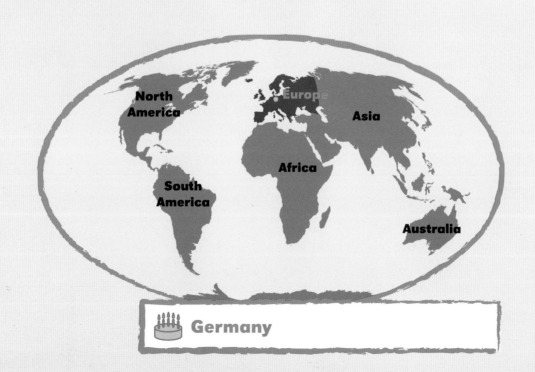

North
America

Europe

Asia

Africa

South
America

Australia

Germany

People open gifts
on their birthdays.
A girl in Mexico picks
which gift to open first.

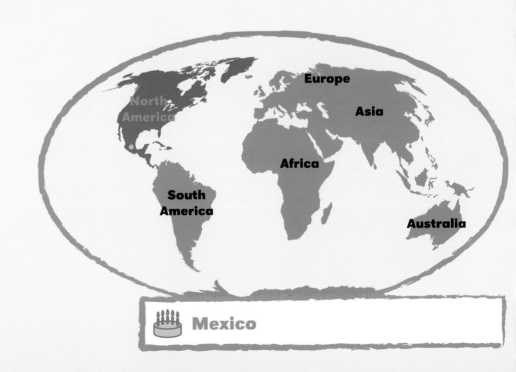

Your birthday

Around the world,
people laugh and play
on their birthdays.
When is your birthday?

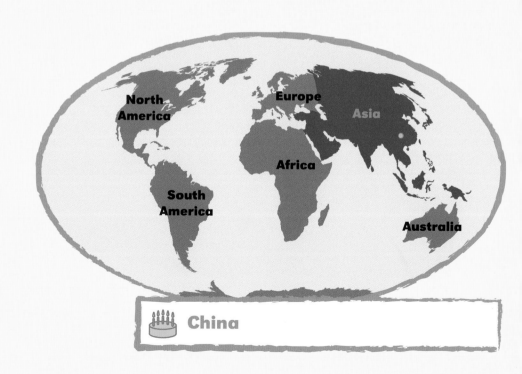

Glossary

celebrate   do something fun, like having a party

culture   way of life, ideas, customs and traditions of a group of people

piñata   container filled with candies and gifts; piñatas are popular at Latin American parties and celebrations

restaurant   place where people pay to eat meals

Find out more

Birthdays Around the World (Engage in Literacy), Jay Dale (Raintree, 2012)

Birthdays Around the World (Bug Club), Lisa Weir (Pearson, 2016)

Birthdays in Different Places (Learning About Our Global Community), Lauren McNiven and Crystal Sikkens (Crabtree Publishing Co, 2016)

Websites

www.birthdaycelebrations.net
Fun facts about birthdays around the world.

www.kidsparties.com/TraditionsInDifferentCountries.htm
Birthday traditions for people in many different countries.

Index